Improving outcomes for children through high quality outdoor provision

EFFECTIVE PRACTICE IN
OUTDOOR LEARNING

TERRY GOULD

If in doubt, let them out!

Published 2012 by Featherstone Education
Bloomsbury Publishing plc
50 Bedford Square, London,
www.acblack.com

ISBN 978-1-4081-456-23

Text © Terry Gould
Design © Lynda Murray
Photographs © Shutterstock 2011, Fotolia 2011

Printed by Martins the Printers, Berwick-Upon-Tweed

This book is produced using paper that is made from wood grown in
managed, sustainable forests. It is natural, renewable and recyclable.
The logging and manufacturing processes conform to the environmental
regulations of the country of origin.

To see our full range of titles visit www.acblack.com

Grateful thanks are offered to all the settings and schools and
resource suppliers who have provided the many images used in
this publication.

Special thanks are extended to: Kids Unlimited Nursery,
Chester; COSY of Derby; Alfreton Nursery School (ANS); Old
Hall Drive Primary School, Manchester; St James CE Primary
School, Manchester; Ringway Primary School, Manchester; St
Margaret Ward RC Primary School, Trafford.

Terry hopes you and your children will enjoy reading the book
and seeing images of your own provision within in it.

Contents

Introduction

Two and three year olds engaging in an archaeological dig close to their nursery.

To some just a pile of logs but to the young child it's a climbing structure or somewhere to look for mini beasts or to play imaginatively.

The real quality of life should not be measured by the number of breaths we take but by the number of times our experiences take our breath away.

(Anonymous)

Research into early brain development has helped us to recognise the important part that movement plays in supporting early learning and development. We now know that physical development opportunities are essential to the cognitive aspects of learning for children and their emotional well being (Bruce & Meggitt, 1999). Nowhere are these physical development opportunities more likely to be available then outdoors.

Outdoor learning spaces are environments where babies and young children learn about the world around them including nature and the seasons. Any judgements we make on the suitability and quality of such spaces should not only reflect the extent to which these are safe and secure for the young child, but also the extent to which these offer challenge and promote exploration, investigation, fun and adventure. An appropriate early years outdoor learning environment within a children's centre, day nursery, school or other setting needs to provide a wide and varied range of challenging and exciting opportunities for children across all areas of learning so as to ensure that …

- their needs are met.

- their ideas and interests are fostered.

- they are able to practise and consolidate their existing skills and develop new ones relevant to their stage of development.

Collecting leaves on an autumn day with a friend.

Using binoculars in a hide outdoors to view a robin close up.

On finding a catkin fallen from a tree the child says to herself "I wonder what it is? Maybe it's a caterpillar?"

Just as with the indoor learning environment, what is provided outdoors should offer children the opportunity to learn in different ways and in different places; so that there is a balance of child-initiated independent play and adult guided/led learning. To achieve this balance, practitioners will need to plan out and present an ever-changing environment which is aimed at meeting the ongoing needs and interests of the young children in their setting.

Using different mediums to dig such as small pebbles (children over three).

Caring for living things and finding out things like "What do snails like to eat?"

Being close to nature might be exploring with a stick in a muddy puddle.

This should focus on the following key aspects:

- Individual children's needs identified from existing information and ongoing observations

- Assessed levels of the skills, understanding and abilities of individual children

- Observed/noted interests of children

There will always be things that appear to 'get in the way of' providing quality, daily outdoor provision, not least of all staffing levels and the weather, but it is about the early years team identifying priorities and turning challenges into opportunities. This will involve thinking creatively, imaginatively and positively about what is provided. The changing and variable weather should be seen as an opportunity, not a barrier, and where necessary a priority should be agreed for the provision of appropriate outdoor clothing. If barriers, such as the weather, are not effectively overcome and turned into positives then outdoor provision will not be what it could and should be. As a result, the entitlement of every child to access daily, quality learning opportunities outdoors will be limited, and their learning and development will be adversely affected.

In today's world the challenge facing all practitioners is to help all children to be as healthy and active as possible. For many children, particularly those in inner city areas, the outdoor area around their home is not as safe as parents/carers would like it to be. So for many young children, outdoor play at home is often restricted. It is therefore even more important for these children that their school/setting provides continuous high quality outdoor play where they can dynamically express their emotions, feeling and ideas; all of which form a key part of their unique personality.

The outdoor environment could and should, inspire the very young child to explore, investigate, create and communicate. At times, the awe and wonder of it should almost feel to them that it 'takes their breath away'.

Chapter 1

An International perspective

In the 21st century, exploring worldwide perspectives are important to us as practitioners responsible for our youngest children because they allow us to reflect on what we are providing in the light of practice in other countries. This chapter will explore perspectives from Italy, Denmark and America.

Reggio Emilia perspective (Italy)

The approach at Reggio Emilia in Northern Italy to learning outdoors focuses on the following significant aspects:

1. The image of the child

2. The expressive arts

3. Progettazione (emergent curriculum or child-centred curriculum)

4. Parents and community relationships

5. The environment

6. Teachers as learners

For these educators, learning outdoors and indoors is about lighting the fires of inspiration not filling the buckets of knowledge.

1 The image of the child

Our image of the child is rich in potential, strong, powerful, competent and, most of all, connected to adults and children.

Loris Malaguzzi

Rather than seeing the child as an empty vessel waiting eagerly to be filled with knowledge, educators at Reggio passionately believe in the concept that a child has unlimited potential and is eager to interact with and contribute to the world. They believe that a child has a fundamental right to 'realise and expand their potential'. For them, a child is driven by curiosity and imagination and delights in taking responsibility for his or her own learning.

Hence for those at Reggio, resources outdoors are as open-ended as possible and children's ideas and thinking are valued and pursued. They have found from this approach that when young children are listened to and given the time and space to express themselves they are capable of achieving in more complex and abstract ways.

Painting on a giant scale observed outdoors at Reggio Emilia.

The famous lions in the local square which inspired creative work by the children.

2 The expressive arts

*The child is made of one hundred.
The child has a hundred languages
A hundred hands a hundred thoughts
A hundred ways of thinking of playing,
of speaking ...*

Loris Malaguzzi

Central importance is given to the expressive arts as a vehicle for learning. Children are encouraged to participate in a variety of expressive activities such as sculpture, dramatic play, shadow play, puppetry, painting, dancing, music, ceramics, construction and writing. These activities take place outdoors or indoors or both, depending on where the children decide they should happen. Initial outside experiences are often taken up by the children as stimuli for things they produce whether this be a working model, a dance, a painting or other formats e.g. The famous poppy artwork.

Teachers believe strongly that imagination plays a key role in the child's search for knowledge and understanding of the world around them. This significantly includes the outdoor environment where children's interest in such things as water fountains and sculptures of lions is supported.

3 Progettazione

It is notoriously difficult to translate, the term 'progettazione' which is often understood to mean emergent curriculum or child-centred curriculum, but the reality is far more complex. Reggio educators talk of working without a teacher-led curriculum but this does not mean that forward thinking and preparation don't take place. Instead they learn to observe children closely, listen to them carefully and give value to their ideas so that they might gain an understanding of what interests children most and create strategies that allow the children to build upon these identified interests.

A trip into the local community to attend an arts festival.

'Topics' for study, which often turn into larger projects, most often come from the children themselves, or sometimes from the educator who knows which subjects naturally interest children or from the family and the wider community. Projects do not follow rigid timetables but rather meander slowly at the pace of the children. Children may be involved in a specific project over a lengthy period of time but not every day; rather returning to it as their interests dictate, revisiting and re-evaluating what they have learned.

Documentation, in the form of photographic and written wall panels, placed at both adult and child height, is a prominent feature of the Reggio Emilia approach.

4 Parents and community relationships

I've learned a lot of things from the infant-toddler centre and pre-school my grandson has attended. They have made me feel alive because I have had to reflect on those values that have always characterised my life. I feel the need to grow with my grandson and this has given me a new outlook on life.

Luciano Gozzi, Grandparent

Reggio educators describe their approach to learning and teaching as a 'pedagogy of relationships' as it is founded on the belief that we learn through making connections between things, concepts and experiences, and that we do so by interacting with other people and with our surrounding environment. This is evident in the key role given to participation at every level: both within the setting (between children and between children and adults) and also between families, the setting and the local community.

5 The environment

A Reggio pre-school is a special kind of place, one in which young human beings are invited to grow in mind, in sensibility and in belonging to a broader community.

Jerome S Bruner, Psychologist

Rather than indoor and outdoor spaces being separate and used for different purposes, the Reggio setting's indoor and outdoor areas are composed of a series of connecting spaces that flow into one another. Rooms open onto a central piazza, mirroring the central meeting places in the town, and children move freely from indoors to outdoors. This type of free access is conducive to participation and interaction and to the general value of openness.

The environment (indoors and outside) is set up to facilitate the thinking and ideas of the children. They are encouraged to work in groups on projects in which they have demonstrated an interest. The outside environment is a source of colour and texture, and plants are widely used in the classrooms as well as in interior and exterior courtyards. This also serves to create a natural link between the inside and outside environments of the school. Fostering a link with the outside environment is important because Reggio educators believe that as the setting is a place of learning and discovery, one space within it cannot be seen as an island.

Outside play areas and equipment are very much in evidence, often with canopies and verandas forming a physical link between inside and out. Through the use of child-built installations such as 'The Amusement Park for Birds' at the Villetta pre-school, the outside becomes a learning centre where children can learn about the elements and physical forces.

Mirrors are used in a variety of ways. Through them children gain an understanding of themselves in relation to their surroundings, a belief that is central to the philosophy of Reggio.

6 Teachers as learners

Staff development is seen above all as an indispensable vehicle by which to make stronger the quality of our interaction with children and among ourselves.

Carla Rinaldi

The municipal education system 0–6 has long been recognised for its approach to the continuing professional development of all educators. Continuing professional development is not about developing teachers' understanding of how to teach but about developing their understanding of how children learn. Teachers are encouraged to understand children's learning processes rather than acquiring skills and knowledge that they then expect children to learn. Research is a fundamental learning strategy for children in the Reggio schools and this is mirrored in the approach to the role of the educator in the learning process and to professional development.

What can we learn from the Reggio perspective?

- An understanding on how children learn best is significantly important in providing the right environment and pedagogy.

- Provision of a wide range of portable and open ended resources that children can manipulate is critical to children being able to follow their interests.

- Following children's ideas and interests, through sustained shared thinking within group situations, can support children's creativity and imagination leading to improved outcomes.

- The expressive arts are an excellent medium for cross-curricular learning and development.

- A close working relationship with parents and the local community supports a high status, shared, sustained and effective vision which ultimately leads to improved outcomes for children. Documentation of children's learning is an important part of this relationship.

- A strong commitment to staff training and development.

- Continuous links between indoor and outdoor spaces are very supportive of the learning opportunities.

- The importance of providing children with space and time to engage with the resources.

The Danish perspective

There is no such thing as poor weather, only poor clothing.

(Anonymous)

The Danish Social Service Act stipulates that pre-school facilities should form part of the total plan for general and preventative measures for children's welfare. It is the general objective to create, in co-operation with the parents, a framework which favours the development, well-being, and independence of children. These measures must ensure children have a normal day, that at the same time gives them security and challenges, and where close links with adults can develop.

Outdoor clothing enables children to learn safely in all weathers.

Danish early years provision emphasises the value and benefits of outdoor learning. There is a famous Danish saying that 'There is no such thing as poor weather only poor clothing.' and this is very much a reflection of their philosophy – that children should be outdoors in all weathers and at one with nature and the seasons. A number of local authorities have established forest and nature kindergartens (børnehaver) where the children spend a great deal of time outdoors all year round, though a cabin is also available in the area.

Unlike the Early Years Curriculum Guidance in the UK, Denmark's pre-school 'curriculum' is just two pages long and there are no formal assessments. Children are given freedom to explore and experiment through outdoor play. Additionally, there is a strong emphasis on those working with young children being highly skilled, experienced and well educated; with the result that 65 per cent of all staff working in Danish early years centres are educated to degree level.

There are no formalised rules regarding observation and monitoring in Danish early years settings, but many educators have an interest in working with interaction-based observations. It is common for settings to hold parent consultations, where the staff of the setting discuss with individual children's parents how their children thrive in the institution, what they occupy themselves with, their strong and weak points, and about their social relationship with other children.

In the past decade many Danish initiatives have been undertaken to increase the participation of children in decision making processes and to give them more influence over their daily lives. One such initiative was a project called 'Children As Citizens'. The purpose of this project was to give children increased opportunities to take part in local activities and decision-making.

Young children are given freedom outdoors.

What can we learn from the Danish perspective?

- The large amount of time spent outdoors in many settings and the consequent affinity with nature and the seasons.

- The design and layout of the outdoor space and its use in all weathers.

- The strong partnership with parents.

- The high qualifications and experience of educators.

- The emphasis on social skills and citizenship.

- The levels of understanding, interest and care taken by architects involved in designing early years buildings and outdoor spaces.

- The provision of special outdoor clothing for all young children.

This initiative had an impact on improved outcomes for the children in terms of being able to make decisions and all this involves. The idea was to give them a say in the actual content of activities as well as the planning and implementation. One of the most important elements in the project was the close relationship established as a result between the children and adults involved. The evaluation of the outcomes of this initiative showed that even very young children are able to make decisions concerning matters which are important to them.

Many Danish architects show a high level of understanding of the correlation between the physical framework and educational work, not only in relation to the actual design and layout of buildings but also in relation to surroundings and outdoor play areas. This has developed over a period of time and many attempt to put themselves in the role of a child to ensure what they design works well for the child.

The American perspective

Across the vastness of America the quality of early years outdoor provision varies greatly but there are many growing pockets of good practice to be found. For example, in Kentucky, the state has taken on board the philosophical stance/understanding that children develop at different rates. As a result of this, children in the kindergarten are grouped, for part of the time, by skills and ability rather than solely by age. This tradition emphasises that the recognition of an individual child's uniqueness and developmental difference is central to defining the curriculum for these children.

Virtually all American states offer some publicly-funded early years pre-kindergarten and/or kindergarten education. Pre-kindergarten children are usually aged four to five, whilst kindergarten caters for five to six year olds. Enrolment in pre-kindergarten and kindergarten education is usually voluntary. Kindergartens are often part of local elementary schools. Community early years day care centres, where they exist, offer full time care for the children of working mothers or whose parents are ill, and the affordably modest fees are kept low by supplementation with private and government funds.

Child development centres might sometimes cater for those disadvantaged areas with state and federal support. The issue of universal access to quality early years provision appears very contentious and is not available in all states. There is no national 'curriculum' for the early years and it is up to each state to decide on their own vision and values and how these are implemented. In the 'Children of America' early years centres, which exist in a wide range of locations (12 states in all) including: Delamere, Illinois, New Jersey, New York, North Carolina, Maryland, Ohio, Wisconsin, Indiana, Pennsylvania and Virginia, teachers work under the 'I am' philosophy to promote each child's physical, social, emotional and intellectual development. The approach concentrates on allowing each child

to learn through their own creativity and self-reliance, while laying the foundation for reading, writing and logical thinking.

Other private early years providers are growing fast like 'Pre-School of America' which is now one of the largest in New York City providing centres in places like the Bronx, Staten Island, Manhattan, Brooklyn & Queens. Here experienced teachers plan thematic units in maths, literacy, science, social studies, art, music and movement to thoroughly prepare children for a smooth transition to kindergarten. Children are helped in making independent choices in a child-centred learning environment. Opportunities for hands-on learning are presented daily, allowing children to grow through an emphasis on play and real world experiences which includes engaging with nature and natural materials outdoors.

There are some states in the USA, for example, Massachusetts, which use 'disciplines' (subject areas) as the structure for their curriculum. In this case, the advantage is continuity, as the same discipline areas are also used as the basis for the curriculum throughout the Massachusetts' education system from pre-kindergarten to grade 12.

The Learningden Pre-school in Santa Barbara, California has chosen to offer provision based on the Reggio Emilia approach. Topics/projects here are driven by 'questions, information and excitement' expressed by the children themselves. Many settings in California, including Learningden, offer a linked outdoor area where there are natural elements of trees, plants and wild grassy areas which offer children the opportunity to experience nature at first hand. Such activities as den building using tree branches and found materials (including opened out cardboard boxes and old blankets), and caring for wildlife are supported and encouraged.

In his book *The Last Child In The Woods* Richard Louv highlights research from around the world, including America, which shows, among other things, that children who do not play outdoors and do not have sufficient contact with natural materials and resources are more likely to develop what he terms 'Nature Deficit Disorder' which makes them more likely to suffer from conditions like depression, attention deficit disorder and obesity.

The local beach is a rich source of natural materials for exploratory play and adventure used by Learningden Pre-school.

Shade and shelter utilised for a group time session outdoors.

What can we learn from the American perspective?

- A recognition that the uniqueness of the child is an important concept.

- There may be advantages in terms of continuity to have the same 'disciplines' across the board from the early years through to secondary.

- Affordability of fees is important for many. The subsidising of fees from government/private funding can help to keep these at affordable levels.

- Natural early years outdoor environments are important as they help to ensure that we don't separate or isolate children from nature and the natural world.

Summary

All three perspectives show us that in places around the world children and outdoors work well together in terms of improving outcomes. They demonstrate that an outdoor space is most effective when it offers challenging and accessible learning opportunities for children, including those which promote and encourage:

THINKING

FEELING

DOING

BEING

ENJOYING

These perspectives also show us that where the outdoors is valued by those who run the education and care systems then it is more likely to also be seen as such by those who work in the system. Of course within these countries there is a wide variance in terms of outdoor provision. For example, the values and quality of provision of the Reggio Emilia area is not taken up across Italy. Indeed, my own recent experience has seen some very limited/poor outdoor pre-school provision in areas less than 100 miles away from Reggio Emilia.

When thinking about why this is so, I have come to the conclusion that it's because many people fail to recognise the value of high quality outdoor provision and that in these cases it's seen to involve extra work and higher costs — facts which are often allowed to become barriers and/or limiting factors.

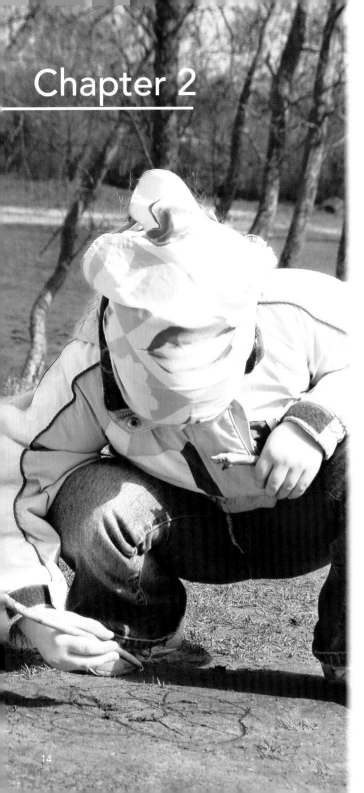

Chapter 2

The importance and value of outdoor learning

Outdoor learning makes a major contribution to children's development. Young children will be missing out on important learning opportunities if quality outdoor provision is not available to them regularly.

Edgington M: *The Nursery Teacher in Action.*
(Sage Publications 2002)

Exploring and having fun in the snow.

Often people question why outdoor learning is so important for the very young child and some will specifically ask 'Why should they learn outdoors?'

We must ensure that everyone involved – parents/carers and practitioners – gain a real understanding of the many great reasons/ benefits for taking play and learning outdoors. Such things as:

Mark making using jumbo chalks.

- Seasonal and weather changes help develop children holistically and encourage specific areas of learning, such as knowledge and understanding of the world.

- All areas of learning and development can be readily supported outdoors. Such important areas as language, mathematics and science can each be supported with hands-on experiences and the chance to work on a larger scale in ways which are bigger, bolder, messier and noisier!

- Children can manage physical risks and test their boundaries in ways they cannot indoors. They can create dens and hiding places and engage in experiences that help develop confidence, creativity, independence and decision-making skills.

- The more children's muscles and senses are exercised, the more the brain develops its capacity for learning.

14

- The outdoor environment has unique characteristics and features that cannot and do not exist indoors. Some things can only be learned about outside e.g. weather, seasons, nature etc.

- Outdoor learning has equal if not greater value than indoor learning.

- Being outdoors can have a positive impact on children's well being and development. They can access the fresh air and space to move in much faster and more complex ways that they need so much.

- The sedentary nature of children's lives and the subsequent increase in overweight children creates an important need for physical activity which generally cannot be achieved indoors.

- Living things can be observed in their natural habitat and nature observed and experienced first hand.

- Outdoor experiences can effectively complement the indoor learning environment through offering activities in more active and exciting ways.

- Outdoor activity can help to reduce behaviour and discipline problems as children are less likely to seek challenges in undesirable, aggressive and unsafe ways.

- Some children are likely to learn more effectively outdoors – particularly those with a more kinaesthetic learning style. Often this is the boys but some girls too!

"Look it's a magpie up there."

Sensory plants add to the learning experience and ambience of outdoors.

Feeling the texture and smelling the scent of the lavender.

Balancing can be a social activity as well as a physical challenge!

But…

- Children need the support of attentive and engaged adults who are enthusiastic about the outdoors and understand the importance of outdoor learning.

- Children need high quality outdoor learning which is enhanced by an environment that is richly resourced with play materials that can be adapted and used in different ways.

Practitioners, parents and children need support in understanding the value of outdoor provision so that they appreciate more fully what Richard Louv as a parent himself concluded from all his research that 'Time in nature is not leisure time it's an essential investment in our children's health'. Settings can support this through having a visible policy on outdoor play which includes such things as:

- appropriate outdoor learning displays;

- outdoor learning workshops for parents;

- exciting activities and opportunities for children;

- evidence in learning journeys/development files of how children are benefitting from their outdoor experiences;

- a setting/school brochure which emphasises the need and the requirement for outdoor learning;

- parents knowing that appropriate all weather outdoor clothing is provided for their children.

The adult role is crucial.

Simple tools provide a real stimulus in this building site set up outdoors.

First hand experiences of growing things on a larger scale are better than any book on growing.

It's true, there is no such thing as bad weather, only poor clothing.

Using the outdoors is almost always about language

Even when children appear to be focusing on the physical or other aspects of play, they often engage in language e.g. in using the fixed climbing structure children talk with each other about what they are doing, or going to do. They say things like "I'm gonna get underneath it. Are you coming with me?" or "Can you get to the top?" and "Come on let's crawl through the tunnel."

When exploring the mini beast area of stones and logs they lift a stone and say "Look look it's a worm... Don't tread on it or it'll die" or "Aw no it's gone under that big stone now!"

Children use language much more outdoors than they do indoors to express their thinking and to communicate what they are actively doing. With the support of a skilful and experienced adult, this can lead to many things including children developing their skills as writers by recording what they see and do.

The fact that there are so many opportunities for language and literacy in the developed outdoor area is what makes it such a potentially rich learning environment. Speaking and listening and reading and writing can all be engaged with through outdoor role-play such as a building site, road works, an outdoor café or a garden centre. A range of signs can be used on a building site such as:

STOP,
GO,
DANGER,
ENTRANCE,
EXIT,
BRICKS,
TIMBER,
CEMENT ROOF TILES,
NO ENTRY etc.

Children might use a sign to stop traffic whilst they move (or pretend to move) equipment or dig a hole. They might read a sign, write their own sign, draw up a labelled plan or write a simple letter. They could create a bill for materials purchased or write down an order taken over the telephone for delivery or collection. The potential appears almost unlimited where there are skilled practitioners on hand to support this through modelling interactions and using language and literacy skills. Through such interactions, children will be developing their use of an increasing range of familiar but also learning some new words.

Outdoor learning and the EYFS themes

Children are offered many opportunities when learning outdoors which support the four EYFS themes. These themes support outcomes for children in a range of different ways. These are good to talk through with staff and parents so as to see how outdoor provision can link to improved outcomes.

A unique child

Outdoors, children are able to…

- be themselves and explore who they are and how they belong;

- learn at their own pace but often in more active, messy and meaningful ways than indoors;

- access the equipment and resources through the way they are designed and presented;

- take pleasure in movement and challenging their physical skills and their own limits;

- be energetic and boisterous and uninhibited in exploring and fanatising;

- holistically think, feel, be and belong in their own time and at their own pace;

- learn to act and respond safely and to keep themselves healthy and safe;

- show a range of different interests than when indoors;

- demonstrate responses to different situations than when indoors.

Positive relationships

Outdoors provides different experiences and challenges of working and playing together thus enabling children…

- to play and work with adults as equals;

- to manage their own play and work with their peers;

- to consider the needs and feelings of others;

- to learn to be aware of the safety of others;

- to develop emotional well being and social skills in a range of different ways;

- to use language to communicate, socialise, have fun, collaborate and communicate on larger and more open scales without being inhibited about being noisy, energetic or messy.

Positive environments

An appropriately developed and resourced environment outdoors helps children:

- to be curious and fascinated by the ever-changing outdoor natural world;

- to be inspired to express their ideas, thoughts and feelings in different ways from indoors;

- to change their environment through open-ended, flexible and versatile resources;

- to learn through play, active engagement, their senses and movement;

- to use a range of tools and equipment that would not be possible indoors;

- to be inspired by the uncertainty of the daily changes which occur spontaneously around them such as the ladybird on the leaf, the fall of snow, the helicopter flying overhead or the fire engine, police car or ambulance, with siren blaring, rushing to an emergency;

- to engage in learning in bigger, bolder, messier and noisier ways.

Learning and development

Outdoor learning enables children to learn different things and/or in different ways such as:

- exploring the weather and seasons first hand;

- digging on a larger scale in soil and sand and other media;

- growing and nurturing a range of plants, flowers and vegetables;

- caring for and nurturing wildlife and kept animals;

- using more frequent, different and often more elaborate language to communicate;

- being in touch with and exploring the natural world;

- working and playing generally on a larger scale;

- meeting their individual and group needs e.g. need for fresh air and vigorous exercise.

19

Key considerations when developing outdoor space

Access to the outdoors is more than a recreational exercise; it offers activities planned to develop skills and confidence across the whole curriculum.

The Select Committee on Education 2001

Most practitioners have a good understanding about the kind of areas they should develop and maintain indoors. However, when it comes to the outdoor area they feel much less knowledgeable about how the space can best be developed so as to maximise the learning and development opportunities it can offer.

When developing any outdoor space one of the most important considerations is about access. Ideally the outdoor space should be directly linked to the indoor space so that children can move freely between the two.

Outdoor spaces come in all sorts of shapes and sizes. Some are full of natural architecture like trees, bushes, plants, flowers and grass whilst others have hard surfacing with little or no natural plants, trees or bushes. In fact, every outdoor space is unique and no two spaces can be developed in exactly the same way. However, there are some guidelines that we can all use which give us insights into how we should develop the space.

The EYFS guidance framework (2007) identifies that outdoors should offer opportunities for children to....

* be energetic, adventurous, messy and noisy;

* talk, listen, interact and make friends;

* imagine, dream, invent, fantasize;

* create, invent, construct and deconstruct;

* investigate, explore, discover, experiment with their own ideas and theories;

* make sounds and music, express ideas and feelings;

* find patterns, make marks, explore different media and materials;

* investigate concepts and ideas;

* be active, run, climb, pedal, jump and throw;

* dig, grow, nurture, cultivate;

* hide, relax, find, be calm, reflect;

* have responsibility, be independent, collaborate with others.

So whatever is provided needs to feature experiences which will promote and facilitate all of this: much of which involves children moving, exercising and developing their physical skills.

Developing physical skills and knowledge involves two major requirements for young children which the practitioner needs to support:

1. Movement and space: Where children learn to move with confidence, imagination and safety, with an awareness of space, themselves and others.

2. Health and bodily awareness: Where children learn the importance of keeping healthy and factors which contribute to their health.

Key considerations – 'The S factor'

In order to ensure that what is provided meets all the identified requirements of the early years, as well as individual children's predicted or identified needs and interests, there are some important aspects, which I shall refer to as 'Key considerations', that need to be thought about at the design/development stage.

These include the following:

1. Surfaces

2. Stimulus

3. Staffing and supervision

4. Storage

5. Seating

6. Shade and shelter

7. Sustainability

8. Safety and security

9. Space

With the above in mind I have termed this group of key considerations the 'S factor' of early years outdoor design.

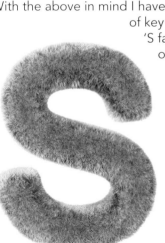

1 Surfaces

- Children benefit from opportunities to move on a range of different surfaces.

- Surfaces can include: tarmac, rubber, concrete, bark chippings, grass etc.

- All surfaces should be risk assessed on an ongoing basis.

- Different surfaces can be introduced e.g. roadway area — rumble strips.

- Very large areas of some surfaces, such as wooden decking and block paving, need careful consideration — particularly where these are in very exposed open spaces. These can suffer from water penetration that allows moss to grow.

This roadway has a rumble strip made out of stone setts.

Hard surfaces like tarmac can support maths based games like skittles.

Hopscotch - a surface marking that provides another stimulus for children.

2 Stimulus

As with the indoor area, stimulus is important for children's learning.

- Some stimulus will be intrinsically provided through the way the area has been planned and developed and will vary with the seasons. Others will need to be provided through a range of resources on a daily/weekly basis.

- Outdoor resources boxes can also be used to provide added stimulus.

- Stimulus will be effectively provided through any planned focused and targeted activities.

- Practitioners will enhance the provision through adding and changing some of the resources in line with children's interests, identified needs and topics from their medium term planning.

- Children will only be able to access some experiences in the outdoor area as these can never be provided indoors e.g. a fall of snow, a puddle, mud etc. These can be used to act as a stimulus for them to talk, listen and think or write about in terms of what they have smelled, seen, heard or touched.

- Outdoor learning experiences provide the opportunities for learning and development on a much bigger scale than indoors. We should not be taking the Lego outdoors!

- First hand experience of the weather and seasons is better than any book.

- Outdoor spaces provide fresh air and more space for children to move than indoors.

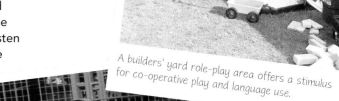

A builders' yard role-play area offers a stimulus for co-operative play and language use.

A chalk board provides a stimulus for mark making.

An outdoor bridge and surrounding space provides a stimulus for playing out stories like *The Three Billy Goats Gruff.*

Growing areas provide a stimulus for caring for plants.

Nature provides stimulus through weather and seasons — in this case snow.

3 Staffing and supervision

An appropriate ratio of staff to children in the outdoor area is important. At no time must very young children be in the outdoor area without adequate adult support/supervision.

- The deployment of staff should be identified in the short term/daily planning.

- All staff should be involved in planning for the outdoor area as well as the indoor area.

- Continuous indoor/outdoor provision is always the required ideal.

- As with the indoor area – with a group of children and two practitioners, one will take on the role of targeter/manager and the other will lead a focused activity.

- The role of the adult is critical to successful outdoor learning. All adults need to have a clear understanding of their own roles and responsibilities.

4 Storage

As you develop/extend the outdoor provision more storage space is needed for the growing range of resources and equipment provided.

- Large shipping type metal containers, or commercially produced metal sheds, fitted with high quality padlocks are the least prone to theft and vandalism. These may in some cases need planning permission. Other options are traditional wooden sheds where the site is safer/more secure.

- Increasingly, settings are using purpose built storage trolleys that can quickly, easily and safely be wheeled in and out. These contain developed *outdoor resource boxes*.

One example of a purpose built outdoor resource trolley. This one is made by Peppertree Designs of Manchester and comes with a lifelong guarantee!

Adults interacting with children can provide a role model for language and sometimes can raise the level of the play.

Heavy duty metal containers or sheds are sometimes needed where vandalism is an issue.

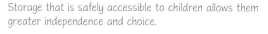

Storage that is safely accessible to children allows them greater independence and choice.

5 Seating

Just as with an indoor area children and adults will sometimes need somewhere to sit.

- Seating can support interaction, imaginative play, sharing books, drawing, writing, speaking and listening.

- Seating can be fixed or portable. Other seating can be brought outdoors as required such as chairs, bench sets, child-sized patio sets etc.

- Some seating will be purpose built such as a bench around a tree or a range of low level seating in a gathering area.

- Other things may be used as seating including old milk crates, large tractor tyres or wood or bricks used to edge growing trees.

6 Shade and shelter

This can be created in a wide variety of ways including:

- Creating open-ended shelters and den making opportunities.

- Child-sized gazebos or similar.

- Providing children with clothing and other equipment which they can use to protect themselves from the weather elements e.g. rainwear suits, sun hats, woolly hats, scarves, gloves, umbrellas, wellingtons, long sleeved tee shirts, sunglasses, sun visors.

- Developing outdoor areas which are partly shaded by the building itself or by planted trees.

- Providing fixed structures such as verandas, canopies, open wooden structures, covered mini seating areas or willow tunnels.

Seating set into the hard surfacing.

Seating fitted around an existing tree.

Tent type structures are affordable, easy to erect and store and provide suitable shelter.

Once established willow tunnels offer a range of opportunities.

More permanent structures can also be built and these will not need any time to get out and put away but do cost money.

Simple den structures are also cheap and easy to erect. This broom stave is set in concrete in a plastic bucket to give more stability to the den.

There are a variety of wooden structures that can be purchased. These can be very useful for all weather shelters and should last for years.

7 Sustainability

At the planning stage, every feature within the outdoor space needs to be designed so as to be fit for purpose.

Features should be able to withstand the daily levels of use for which they were intended, as well as for all the extra uses which children will invent!

Leadership and management will need to consider that:

- Outside working hours vandalism and abuse of outdoor features may be a problem.

- Materials should be as durable as possible and if timber is used it should be of a heavy duty type and rot resistant treated.

- Designs with maintenance in mind should improve sustainability.

- Wherever possible low maintenance designs are preferable. This is particularly relevant for large planted areas where block planting of one species will simplify maintenance schedules.

- Existing features such as trees and slopes should be made use of wherever possible.

8 Safety and security

- In the outdoor area, safety and security is essential for children's well being.

- Practitioners need to think carefully about everything they provide.

- Risk assessments should take place where this is seen as necessary/desirable.

- The outdoor area needs to have secure fencing, which offers a protective perimeter. This should be high enough not to be easily climbed over and where possible offering the opportunity to see through.

- Any gated entry points need to be secure and unable to be opened other than by practitioners during sessions.

- Safety checks should always take place before each session to ensure there are no hidden dangers from:

  (i) Faulty equipment;

  (ii) Dangerous materials, such as needles, glass etc which may have found its way into the area;

  (iii) Things growing in the area which present a hazard such as brambles or toadstools.

- Children need to be taught to keep themselves safe and secure when using the outdoor area – including staying in the shade on excessively hot days.

- Being safe in their play is a child's entitlement. This does not mean that young children will never be allowed to take risks or that accidents will never happen.

- If children injure themselves we need to know that all reasonable steps were taken to make it as safe as possible through ongoing risk assessment.

- Regular bi-annual safety/maintenance checks of equipment (ideally by outside agents) should take place.

- Whether it is trips out or having visitors in or a daily setting-based activity, practitioners should risk assess new situations as well as any others they are unsure about.

- Children need to be shown how to use equipment and resources safely including how to keep themselves and others safe.

Secure bolts and locks on gates are essential. Labels on gates are important too and also offer an opportunity for children to read.

9 Space

- Spaces need to be laid out and divided to support the activities safely.

- Thought needs to be given as to where each of the developed outdoor areas are best sited.

- Some areas will need more space than others and these should be planned for at the outset.

- Thought should be given to where best to site an outdoor water tap and/or barrel.

- The outdoor space/s should be easily accessible from indoors so as to facilitate continuous indoor/outdoor provision.

- Thought should also be given to supervision of the areas. Hence any dividing fencing between developed areas should be a maximum of 1 to 1½ metres high and ideally children should be able to see though it. Many such dividing fences can also host activities.

Fencing between areas should be low level.

All settings need an outdoor tap (at child height) or a water barrel – but having both is the ideal.

Chapter 4

Areas for development outdoors: towards a design brief

Outdoor environments are places where babies and young children are learning about the wider world, and assessments of these spaces should not only judge the extent to which they are safe but should also reflect how they provide challenge and promote adventure and exploration, even for the youngest children.

Abbott, L and Langston, A. (2005). Birth to Three Matters. Open University Press

The following guidelines about 15 different areas are provided to support planning and development of an outdoor area for children aged 2-5 years. The first four areas identified will take up the most space and should be the first areas entered into any design. NB: In many outdoor spaces of a limited size it will not be possible to have all of the 15 areas and therefore some will have to be amalgamated, missed out or rotated daily/weekly according to the needs of the children in your setting.

With younger children such as babies and very young toddlers the areas and space will often be more limited and will mainly involve things to support their physical/sensory exploration and investigation needs. The nature and safety of outdoor surfaces will need to be carefully considered and where possible some grass should be offered for them to crawl on as well as soft surfacing.

An outdoor space for babies. This setting plans to introduce a small grass area and some rubberised soft surfacing next year.

1 The roadway area

This area will provide a simple or complex road system (subject to space and children's stage of development) allowing children the opportunity to enjoy a range of imaginary, sensory and physical activities (push, pedal, ride and overtake) make decisions, find routes and role-play.

Tyres create a feature in the turning circle.

A rumble strip of inset logs adds a sensory dimension and helps to slow the traffic down!

This portable bridge adds another level of challenge.

Planting up a tyre enhances the roadway.

A roadway built on an incline that offers challenge and interest.

A close up of a rumble strip.

2 The running and ball play area

This area provides children with opportunities for running, developing ball skills, dancing, skipping and enjoying the space. This can also be used for organised group activities which need space, e.g. parachute play, dance sessions etc. Ideally it should be flat and level. This area can have surface marking to enhance games such as number snake or hopscotch.

Superhero play.

Space to kick or throw balls.

Parachute play.

3 The climbing and adventure area

This area will incorporate fixed equipment and/or space where appropriate portable equipment may be used. It offers physical development opportunities through fixed and portable climbing and children will be able to climb, swing, crawl, hide, balance and experience height.

Traversing tower.

Inset tyre balancing set up — new tyres half set into the ground.

A balancing structure.

An A-frame climbing structure. Slides are not recommended by physiotherapists — offer more challenging structures, like netting.

A beam for hanging/swinging.

Fixed low level balancing beams that can double up as seating.

A challenging and very effective balancing area.

4 The natural area

An entirely natural area of bushes, trees and shrubs (with pathways through) and spaces which offer the opportunity to investigate, design, explore, experiment and construct using natural materials. This area will enhance children's sense of adventure, make believe, fun and enjoyment, e.g. in den building. Where space is limited this area may be represented by trees and bushes planted across the outdoor space. It may well include willow domes or structures.

A den using camouflage netting.

Trees provide natural architecture.

A willow dome.

A willow tunnel (also used as part of a roadway).

A mini forest of silver birch trees.

An area designed and built around the existing trees.

A natural area with secret spaces to hide and play.

Planted up tyres.

5 | The digging area

This area provides children with the opportunity to dig using a range of tools and to explore natural materials including soils, stones, and living things such as worms and other mini-beasts. The area does not need to be too large but should be big enough for up to three or four children to use at any one time. Ideally, the digging area will be surrounded on at least two sides with hard surfacing.

Digging areas don't have to be huge for younger children.

Using small trowels and forks for digging, ready to plant.

6 | The planting out and growing area

This area will provide a range of opportunities for children to grow plants, vegetables and flowers and to learn about looking after them. Ideally, this area will be sited close to a water supply, e.g. an outdoor tap and/or a water butt.

Raised growing beds areas offer a quick solution to this setting's outdoor growing needs.

Potatoes growing in a wooden barrel

7 The wildlife area

This should be a clearly defined area that is allowed to become wild and which is planned and planted to attract a variety of wild life into the grounds, enabling children to have a range of opportunities to observe, enjoy and learn.

8 The natural materials area

This area will provide opportunities for large-scale experimentation, exploration and imaginative play with a range of natural materials including sand, water, large pebbles, different-sized logs, pinecones, large shells, etc.

A log structure to attract mini beasts.

Buddleia bushes are cheap to buy, quick and easy to grow and attract butterflies and bees.

A bird table among some small bushes and plants.

Water play with guttering and holders.

A simple but effective outdoor sand pit that has an elasticated cover at night to keep the cats and foxes out.

Natural materials.

Jugs, funnels and pipes make great water play resources.

9 The creative/sculpture/model making area

This area will provide resources, equipment and materials which support a range of opportunities for children to work on a large scale. This will include painting, drawing, sculpting, making large models and woodworking.

Chalking on large fixed board and then using water soaked rollers to wash off.

Painting with a roller on large fixed wall board.

Painting on a larger scale.

Weaving using the back of a bread crate fixed to the fence.

10 The sitting, reading and gathering area

This area provides children with the space to enjoy storytelling, reading books, talking, engaging in quiet reflection, and listening to taped stories, music or poetry. Children can also use this area to talk and socialise.

An adult sharing a book with a child.

A planter doubles up as a seat.

A storyteller's chair and wooden benches make this a desirable location for groups.

Woven willow tunnels make a superb gathering place that can be sited in different outdoor areas.

11 The sensory/sounds area

This area provides opportunities for children to experience a range of sensory stimulation. They are able to experiment with making sounds using larger and different 'musical instruments' e.g. bin lids fixed to walls, large oil drums, home-made instruments, large manufactured instruments (floor xylophones wind chimes etc.) and also experience a range of sensory stimulation from natural and made resources, plants and materials.

Large floor xylophone

A sensory 'musical' washing line.

Old CDs hung on a tree reflect the light and move in the wind.

These sunken plastic pipes can be struck to create music.

Sensory plants, such as rosemary and chives, in a wooden tub.

12 The imaginative play area

Although children will play imaginatively in all areas outdoors, having an area dedicated to imaginative play in its own right will offer children the chance to engage in purposeful, larger scale, outdoor role-play and related construction activities using a range of materials and resources.

"Oh yes and what did you see happen then?"

The joiners are here with their tools. "What shall we build for you?"

Simple resources, yet complex play.

It's those superheroes again - this time off on a make believe ship.

13 The mini beast area

This area will provide opportunities for children to investigate and find out first hand about mini beasts.

A minibeast hunt under the log in the long grass.

Children enjoy digging almost anywhere!

Children are fascinated by minibeasts outdoors.

14 Construction and building area

This area will provide opportunities for children to build with a range of resources and equipment on a larger scale than indoors e.g. den making.

It's amazing the den you can make with just a few covers and an archway.

Building with Bau Play. The bigger the things to build with outdoors the better.

15 Performing arts area

This area will allow children opportunities to sing songs and rhymes and/or to perform small made up shows.

Every child painted a pebble that was then concreted in and so they all helped to create this performance circle.

A simple pallet like structure makes a great mini stage to sing on.

A fixed stage structure that's great for lots of other things too like group times.

Chapter 5

Outdoor resources and activities

The best outdoor provision takes...

an approach to outdoor learning that considers experiences rather than equipment

and in this way...

places children at the centre of the provision being made.

(EYFS Guidance 2007)

Outdoor resources loosely fall in two distinct groups:

- Those which are fixed

- Those which are moveable/portable

An effective outdoor area needs an appropriate amount of both fixed and moveable/portable items.

Fixed items need to be as open-ended as possible in the ways they can be used by children.

When providing additional resources and equipment you should always consider what can be done almost immediately by using low/minimum cost resources. Other developments and resourcing will take more time and cost that bit more.

On the following pages are some examples at three different costing levels.

Key Resources

1 **Cost:** Low/minimum (Free up to £50)
Timing: Definitely almost immediately

These could include:

- Large/medium sized logs
- Outdoor tap/outdoor water butt
- Blankets, ropes, pegs, sheets, carpet and card tubes
- Cardboard boxes
- Bubble pots
- Ribbons, raffia strips of material and weaving frames
- Natural materials such as mini logs, acorns, pine cones, leaves and shells
- Planted up recyled containers e.g. old buckets and tubs
- Gutters, pipes and funnels
- Carpet tiles
- Found/recycled resources (to use for den making) such as old blankets or sheets, carpet roll, card inners, pegs, strings and bamboo poles
- Pipes funnels and gutters for water play
- Milk/bread/beer crates
- Outdoor dressing up clothes/ materials (charity shops are a good source for these items)

- Gardening tools including watering cans (many suitable items can be purchased from the £1 shop – however care needs to be taken to ensure these are safe and suitable)
- Smaller car tyres to roll or bus/ tractors tyres to plant up
- Hoops
- Old CDs to hang from the trees
- Bats and balls
- Outdoor resource boxes (see section below for ideas)

Most often this can cover portable resources or resources for a specific area or to attend to a specific feature which is dangerous or in poor condition.
This might be things like:

- Wooden/bark chippings to spread over a really muddy area or pathway
- Raised beds that have fallen into misuse to be cleared and replanted

2 **Cost:** Medium (£50-£500)
Timing: Probably over a few months

These could include:

- Woodwork bench and tools
- Willow-woven tunnels
- Two person trikes
- Wigwams
- Gazebos
- Raised growing beds
- Fixed wall boards for chalking, drawing and painting
- Fixed wooden bridge

- Fixed rubber matting seeded with grass (e.g. in muddy area)
- Wooden seating
- Small scale planting
- Outdoor sandpit
- Additional/replacement hidey cubes
- Child-sized parachute
- Seater/planters

3 **Cost:** Higher (£500+)
Timing: Possibly within 1-2 years

These could include:

- Climbing structures e.g. climbing frames, traversing towers
- Wooden shelter-type structure, raised from the ground with wooden floor
- Large living willow tunnel/s or dome
- Higher exterior fencing
- Storyteller's chair and seating
- Veranda and shutters

- Complex roadway
- Large sunken sandpit
- Large scale planting of trees, bushes, plants
- Large scale ground works e.g. hard resurfacing, drains
- Gathering structure with overhead covering/roof

Outdoor resource boxes

Children need a wide range of portable resources appropriate for daily continuous provision which will supplement and enhance those items which are permanently fixed. A range of resource boxes, purchased at minimum cost, should include some of the following:

- Book box

  Suggested contents to include a small selection of fiction and non-fiction books linked to the topic, books relating to the outdoor environment and weather, books made with the children relating to the outdoor environment/provision, small padded seating/cushions and small blankets.

- Weather/cold day box

  Suggested contents to include a range of warm hats, gloves and scarves, lined boots and cagoules.

- Gardening/planting box

  Suggested contents to include child-sized hand trowels, forks, sieves, gardening gloves, watering cans, clip boards, pencils, plastic planting label sticks and plastic labels.

- Barbecue role-play box

  Suggested contents to include metal rod type cooking top, range of pretend food, pretend fuel, barbecue cooking utensils, range of plates, cups and eating utensils and small outdoor blanket.

- Maths games box

  Suggested contents to include several large rubber dice, jumbo chalks, bean bags of different colours and shapes, sets of skittles and balls of different sizes, set of number mats to 10, clipboards, pencils and paper.

- Writing box

  Suggested contents to include jumbo chalks, clipboards, paper and chunky pencils, felt tip board markers, portable dry wipe boards, chunky paint brushes and water pots.

Ideas for other outdoor resource boxes

- Role-play box

  e.g. princes and princesses, garage, car wash, firefighters, garden centre, laundry, vets, builders etc.

- Sunny day box
- Picnic box
- Rainy day box
- Mystery box
- Windy day box
- Fabric box
- Water play box
- Den making box
- Natural materials box

Some practical ideas for activities outdoors

A variety of experiences and adult-led and child-initiated activities across all seven areas of learning and development for different stages/ages of children should be provided daily.

Many of these may have a specific focus or purpose but will most often cover several or all the identified areas of learning.

Role-play

Ideas can cover:

- Garden centre
- Car wash
- Barbecue
- Builder's yard
- Laundry
- Vets
- Taxi office
- Archaeology site
- Fire station
- Drive-in cafe or shop

Mathematics

Ideas can include:

- Growing seeds

  Fill a tray with compost, count and sow seeds in individual sections and place it in a sunny sheltered spot. Measure the seedlings as they grow, and use mathematical language to compare size.

- Large cardboard box play

  Undo several boxes at the ends and join together with tape. Talk about the properties of 3D boxes. The children can have fun crawling through the tunnel which can be as long as the number of cardboard boxes available. Develop the vocabulary of under, over, through, out etc.

- Collecting and counting activities

  Hang or place objects on bushes, fencing, walls etc and ask children to collect as many of the same kind of objects as they can e.g. paper plates, pine cones, giant leaves, plastic flowers etc. Then count how many they have collected.

- Matching games

  Place a variety of small pieces of coloured paper or card in a feely box. Ask each child to take a piece from the box and go and find something natural outdoors that almost exactly matches the colour on the card/paper.

Other ideas

- Skittle games
- Teddy bear's picnic
- Numbered carpet tiles and other number line activities
- Measuring height of plants etc.
- Maths trails
- Large boards and chalk

For more ideas on maths outdoors see *The Little Book of Maths Outdoors* by Terry Gould (Featherstone).

Investigation and exploration

Ideas can include:

- **Mini beast hunts**

  Find a rock or log to turn over. What kind of insects can the children see? What patterns in the dirt can they find? Compare sets of creatures, number of legs etc. Keep a record of mini beasts found e.g. over a week and make a graph. Consider making a non-fiction reference book about mini beasts.

- **Bird hides**

  Build a bird hide using camouflage net and den building materials (or just a giant cardboard box). Weave some leafy branches through the net to create extra camouflage. Decorate in earthy colours. Fill the bird feeders, hang them up, go in the hide, stay quiet and wait for birds to visit the feeders. Use bird books/posters to identify any visitors. Draw what you see and 'write' its name. Encourage children to use problem solving skills when creating the bird hide.

- **Exploring shadows**

  On a sunny day, place a doll or teddy on the ground and draw around its shadow. During the day repeat the process with other teddies, dolls and children.

- **Sensory mixtures with different smells**

  Work individually or in pairs to fill a small jug or small container with samples of natural materials found in the environment e.g. petals, grass, moss, mint/peppermint plant leaves, bark etc. Place a hand over the top of the jug/container and shake the contents. Each 'cup full of nature' will have a unique aroma. Use language of capacity e.g. empty, half full, full. Compare and describe the smell of each smelly cocktail with others!

- **Large remote control cars**

  Children to chalk a roadway and then see if they can control the car to go along it.

Other ideas

- Caring for plants e.g. watering

- Growing vegetables and flowers

- Treasure hunts

- Metal detectors

- Wind-up radios and torches

- Playing with natural materials e.g. sand

- Digging

- Fishing game with mini ice cubes with common/natural objects inside

- Simple pulleys

Creative

Ideas can include:

- Musical art activities

  Play different styles or moods of music to the children and encourage them to create a picture with chalks on the ground or on large sheet/s of sugar paper as they listen to the music. (NB Chalks dipped in water will give more vibrant results.) Identify shapes and patterns created during the process.

- Finding pictures in the clouds

  Lie on your back and talk with the children. See what they think they can see patterns of in the clouds – maybe it's an elephant or a giraffe or a car or a person or a bird?

- Weaving ribbons, raffia or willow twigs

  Provide a range of resources suitable for weaving and encourage children to thread through a weaving frame to create patterns.

- Musical washing line

  Hang a range of metal kitchen pots and pans on a washing line and encourage the children to 'play' them while singing a favourite tune.

Other ideas

- Mixing colours to match plants/leaves
- Bark rubbings
- Larger scale modelling
- Outdoor band
- Streamer making
- Kite making
- Making potions
- Making potato dough

Writing/mark making/painting

- Map making

  Bury 'gold treasure' in a large sand pit. Hide the 'gold' in the sand tray, digging area or around the outside area for children to find using a metal detector to help them. Count how many pieces of 'gold' are found and match with the correct numeral on the outdoor number line.

- Spray painting

  Attach a long sheet of paper to the fence or lay it on the ground. Give the children a choice of spray or squeezy bottles with watered down paint (not too thin). Encourage them to spray this on the sheet and make great designs. Children may choose to make marks to include numerals and letters.

Provide a range of larger brushes and pots with water for children to do 'magic' writing and drawing on paving stones.

Other ideas

- Large wall or floor based painting or drawing
- Chalking on hard surfacing
- Squirting and spraying e.g. using washing up liquid bottles and sprays
- Twigs/sticks in mud
- Splash painting
- Making number plates for wheeled toys e.g. bikes
- Paint tracks using tyres

Physical

Ideas can include:

- Washing doll's clothes

  Ask children to fill a large washing up bowl full of bubbly water and suggest they wash the doll's dirty clothes and hang them on a mini washing line. Talk about the language of capacity. How many containers does it take to fill the washing up bowl? Children can be asked to suggest how they think the doll got so dirty!

- Boat races

  Using two pieces of guttering with end caps secured, fill with water and have boat races with jumbo straws to blow the boats along. This activity could be extended by providing other objects which float such as feathers, leaves, corks etc.

- Ball games

  Hang a basket from the branch of a tree and encourage the children to aim sponge balls or other soft objects at the basket. Count how many balls go in/out of the basket, keep a tally chart, use mathematical language such as more than, less than. Make a list of names and scores.

- Balancing course

  Invite the children to build themselves a balancing course using old tyres, crates, small planks etc. Talk about things that might be included. Encourage children to talk about their ideas and maybe draw a sketch/plan.

- The assault course (to build imaginatively and safely)

  Build a course using things like scrambling nets, canes, cones, hoops etc. Give/model some instructions to follow directions such as balancing, jumping over, crawling under. Take a teddy on a journey through the assault course, using positional language as you go. Take pictures of teddy and use these to make into a group book.

Other ideas

- Digging
- Obstacle courses
- Sit on space hoppers/bouncers
- Trikes, bikes, cars and scooters
- Hidey hole cubes and connectors
- Parachute activities
- Climbing activities
- Action songs/rhymes

Language

Ideas can include:

- Making large and small bubbles

Make up a bubble solution and pour into a shallow circular tray. Transform a wire coat hanger into a bubble 'wand'. Wrap wool around the wand (same action as making a pom-pom) and use insulating tape for the 'handle' until smooth. Bend two more coat hangers into (i) a square, (ii) a diamond shape. What shape bubbles do they produce? Use large sweeping movements to create giant bubbles. Talk about your observations.

- Outdoor story based activities

Read a story about a dragon. Use cardboard to make a dragon's head and attach it to a length of material. Cut zig-zags in the edges of the material and decorate with streamers/scales. Decide how many children will fit under the material to make the dragon's body and then the dragon can parade through the outside area in response to suitable music.

- Digital cameras

Children capture images of what they like when they are outside e.g. people, equipment and resources, the garden with bushes, plants and trees, shadows of people etc. The photographs are printed, laminated and used to line the inside of an outdoor den. Children are able to view the photographs and discuss them in detail.

- Puddle play

Encourage the children to experiment with a range of materials to add into puddles – paint, glitter, spaghetti etc. This activity can be enjoyed regularly if children have the opportunity to experiment with a different thing each time. The possibilities are extensive. Invite children to talk about their discoveries. Can they create a pattern in the puddle?

- Growing potatoes

Ask the children to stuff a tyre with newspaper, so reducing the amount of compost needed. Fill it with compost and potatoes and water it well. When the shoots are about 2cms long, put another tyre on top and fill with compost. Repeat until you have a stack of tyres.

At harvest time, help the children remove the tyres one by one and watch the potatoes cascade around them! Throughout the process, allow children opportunities to count, sort, measure, compare size, quantity etc. Take photographs at each stage, make a book and encourage children to tell/write the story. Place the book in the book area to enable children to revisit their learning.

- Hide and seek games

One child is the robot who pretends to be asleep while everyone else hides. Then everyone shouts 'Wake up robot'. Robot wakes up and tries to find the other children. Children take turns to be the robot.

> **Other ideas**
>
> - Performing arts area/ platform
> - Mini megaphones
> - Treasure hunts
> - Phonic/word hunts
> - Follow my leader activity
> - 'Simon says' type games
> - Acting out stories e.g. Going on a Bear Hunt or The Three Billy Goats Gruff or Chicken Licken
> - Ring games
> - Two-way walkie-talkies

Social and self care

Ideas can include:

- Co-operative wheeled toys

Set up the activity where children can co-operate using a pull along cart with passenger/s.

- Picnics

Set up a teddy bear's picnic where children have to join in with their own teddy to enjoy a picnic with party food and party games.

- Cold day box

Encourage and support children in selecting items they need to wear to keep warm outdoors from a box containing a range of gloves, hats, scarves etc.

- Chinese new year dragon dance

A number of children stand underneath a blanket (in a row) whilst other children beat drums and/or other instruments. The children under the blanket dance/ move like a dragon across the play area to the music.

> **Other ideas**
>
> - Running games to raise the children's heart beats which they them can feel and talk about
> - Range of resources to choose from and put away
> - Turn taking activities
> - Putting on and taking off coats and outdoor clothing

Chapter 6

Practitioners and parents outdoors

The success of outdoor play rests with the staff. It is only when the whole staff support and enjoy outdoor play that it will work.

Bilton, H. Outdoor Play in the Early Years (2002)

The role of the practitioner

The role of the practitioner is critical to effective learning taking place outdoors.

Practitioners need to have and to display:

- A positive attitude towards outdoor provision.

- An understanding of how children learn.

- An understanding of the importance of including all children in opportunities for outdoor learning.

- A willingness to attend relevant training and put this into practice.

All practitioners working with children outdoors also need to:

- Ensure that all children can access the outdoor curriculum provided and be aware of those children who may need encouragement or support to go outdoors and participate in the full range of activities offered.

- Observe children engaged in activities and use these observations to identify learning needs and plan the next steps for children's learning through providing rich, stimulating and challenging situations for children to experience.

- Respond to children's interests, patterns of behaviour and cultural diversity.

- Act as a role model.

- Extend and develop children's language, communication and thinking skills.

Adults positively engaging with children

Planting and watering seeds together

The quality of the outdoor environment, the time spent outdoors and the learning and development of the children outdoors reflects both on the management of the setting and those working as practitioners in the early years. It is a key aspect of the provision and as such where it is of a less than desirable level it will be a limiting factor for Ofsted judgements which will then be reflected in their assessment of the quality of leadership, management and overall effectiveness of the setting.

When outdoors, practitioners should at various times be:

- Interacting with children.

- Making observations of children which then lead into the next steps in their learning and development.

- Keeping a watchful eye on children ensuring they are safe and are engaging appropriately with the resources.

- Extending children's thinking by the use of open-ended questions such as 'What might happen if?' 'How could you..?' 'When do you think it is best to....?'

- Supporting children's language skills by modelling appropriate language and engaging children by using language.

- Supporting children's social and emotional skills in a range of ways.

- Helping children to keep themselves safe and healthy.

- Modelling appropriate behaviour and use of resources.

Outdoors, children seem to learn more intensely by following their own lines of enquiry, but they still need adult support when working through their thought processes. For example, children who are not able to vocalise their thoughts and feelings on the subject of their explorations need to be supported with a rich vocabulary from adults.

There is a fine line, however, between intervention and interference so that practitioners are able to build on children's interests without imposing their own adult agenda.

Supporting what the child wants to do by holding the wood and part of the tape.

Asking children open-ended questions like 'What does it smell like?'

Interacting with children as play leader

Involving parents/carers

Sometimes, getting parents to see the value of being outdoors can be a challenge. They are naturally anxious about their children's welfare and safety when outdoors and some may even say they do not want their children playing outdoors in wet or cold weather.

Parents/carers need to be supported to have a clear understanding of what their children are learning in the setting and how this is best achieved, including that outdoors. The children's progress and achievements should be shared regularly with parents and details of ongoing attainment provided. Practitioners need to promote to parents the value and nature of the positive learning experiences that the outdoor environment can provide. Parents/carers need to help in understanding the way that children develop and learn and how the outdoor environment impacts on this.

Make sure that parents are fully aware of your policy of encouraging children to play and learn outdoors. Where you have purchased outdoor clothing let them know this and that whatever the weather you will be giving them daily continuous outdoor provision opportunities. Let them know the unique experiences outdoors can offer and why outdoor learning is so important to their child. This will help parents to understand that they need to send their child into the setting with appropriate clothing for outdoor play and learning e.g. shoes not slippers!

Parents/carers should be informed regularly on key aspects of the provision/curriculum, so that they have the opportunity to share their own knowledge, skills and experiences and be fully involved in decisions about their children's learning and development. It is essential that information is accessible to all parents/carers through newsletters, photo albums, notice boards etc. It is also important to ensure that information is available, where appropriate, in their home languages. Ways in which parents/carers can support their children's learning outdoors at home is also useful to share and much of this could be included in newsletters or a parent's notice board.

An outdoor play parent's notice board sited in a prominent place.

Address parent's concerns about outdoor play positively, but sensitively. Practitioners should re-assure parents that risk assessments have taken place and any dangers minimised but also let them know that children need opportunities for challenges, have to learn about taking risks and that we cannot, nor should we, 'wrap them up in cotton wool' so to speak. Explain that playing outdoors can also provide many opportunities for developing essential life skills. It may be useful to invite the local community nurse to talk to your parents to allay their fears and to explain facts such as children…

- Do not catch colds from being outdoors providing they have appropriate clothing to wear and that they keep active.

- Gain huge physical and mental benefits from being in the outdoor space including the fresh air it offers.

- Are strongly supported in their personal, social and emotional development when they are outdoors.

- Will be developing their gross motor skills outdoors which will later greatly help with their development in the physical aspects of becoming young writers. See The Little Book of Gross Motor Skills (Featherstone).

Practitioners need to understand that for some parents there may be cultural reasons why they do not value outdoor play and learning. Whilst continuing to respect opinions and beliefs we do need to take them on the journey with us for the benefit of their child/ren and come to some agreement where their child/ren are able to benefit as much as possible from outdoor experiences. This might involve:

- Sharing with all parents the resources and materials provided outdoors – perhaps during the induction/transition visits being made with their child.

- Making a book/folder on learning outdoors at your setting available to parents.

- Providing a large display outlining the learning that takes place outdoors and why it is a statutory requirement of the EYFS that quality outdoor learning opportunities are provided every day for all children.

- Providing a large parent's notice board/display board with photos of children really enjoying their outdoor play with explanations of the benefits they are experiencing.

- Language may be a barrier to communicating the benefits of outdoor play to some families. You may overcome these difficulties by, where possible, using staff who speak the same language to talk to families about what their child enjoys doing outside, including signage and photos outdoors that reflect the languages used and the varied cultures in your setting.

- Organise an outdoor cooking event. This will appeal to some families who have not previously taken part in events at your setting – most families view cooking and mealtimes as a valuable social occasion.

- As your parents become more knowledgeable about why their children need to be outdoors and how this is supported at the setting then they will generally become more supportive of this. Indeed, very often it will lead them to reflect on what they could provide for their children outdoors at home.

- Your role will be to inspire them and to support them to use their local park, nature reserve, woods or their own back garden or other spaces with their child.

Engaging parents in this way with outdoor play, will help to ensure that they value it as an essential part of their child's daily life and not an optional extra. Such an effective partnership with parents will support the enrichment of their child's health, well being, learning and development that will have a positive and lifelong impact. One excellent way to encourage greater partnership is to invite and recruit parents/grandparents to come in and help with outdoor provision. As many early years settings tend to be female-dominated, encouraging dads or grandads to become involved is an ideal way to do this as well as providing your boys with positive male role models. Some ideas that dads might be asked to help with could include:

- Manual jobs in your outdoors, such as clearing the growing area

- Leading a ball game (football or skittles etc.) with a small group.

- Supporting children in using large construction materials or making dens.

- Joining in with the role-play such as 'Garden centre' or 'Builder's yard'.

But don't think that some of your mums will not be just as interested or just as good at these things as well!

Parents working with children at the school/setting can help to inspire children and support parent's understanding

Chapter 7

Planting and growing outdoors

There was a time, many years ago when some of the plants, bushes and trees planted in early years outdoor spaces were at the best unsuitable, or at the worst highly dangerous. In my own time as a practitioner I have had to remove such things as roses, bushes with large thorns and trees with dangerous berries or seeds from young children's outdoor spaces.

There are many reasons that you may want to maintain or introduce plants into the grounds of your setting. Some of the main reasons practitioners identify are:

- aesthetic reasons

- sensory experiences

- to encourage wildlife

- screening views such as neighbouring buildings or bin stores

- to reduce pollution, wind and the perception of noise

- to use in the formal and informal curriculum.

Deciding where and when to plant

Once you have decided why you want to plant you will need to work out the best places for the planting to take place. Some places will be obvious e.g. positioning along a boundary fence or climbing plants up a pergola or trellis, whilst others will need more thought.

Issues you may need to consider

Bees and wasps

Don't place plants that will attract insects near to windows — they may fly in on hot summer days.

Keeping things accessible and safe

Make sure planting doesn't block pathways etc. now or in the future. Don't plant things where they will grow and obscure windows later. Think about the ultimate size of the plants you are putting in. When planting trees make sure that they are not going to cause easy access over a security fence when they are large enough to climb.

Some trees, such as some willows, have root systems that reach out far and wide to find moisture. These can therefore cause problems with drains. Large trees can also cause problems of subsidence if planted too close to buildings. If in doubt, especially on clay soils, talk to your local arboricultural officer.

Unsafe berries, bulbs and fruits

Be aware of berries and other fruits. Some are safe to eat, whilst others can cause a range of effects – some very serious. Children are keen to explore the world around them and will pick up tasty looking berries and put them in their mouths. As some berries can be eaten safely, it is not always easy for children, or adults, to know what is poisonous and what is not.

Some bulbs are also poisonous. Whilst not often eaten, some can be mistaken for onions, so care should be taken if they are being stored awaiting planting.

For those seeking an authoritative text *Poisonous Plants and Fungi* by Marion R Cooper and Anthony W Johnson. (Published by HMSO) is one to consider. This book contains an extensive list of plants and fungi that may cause poisoning and other harmful effects.

Deciding what to plant

Once you have decided why you want to plant and where you are planning to place the bushes, trees and plants, you will need to decide upon the appropriate species. Often groups of plants in pots are a useful addition to the area.

Calendula

Lavender

Curry plant

Sweet pea

Nasturtium

Clematis

Wild strawberry

There are a wide range of resources and people who can help you with this depending on your reason for planting – including advisors, other professionals and knowledgeable amateurs.

Here are a few plant species that you might wish to consider:

- Pot Marigold (*Calendula*): bright orange daisies that are easy to grow from seed.

- Sunflowers (*Helianthus annuus*): a bright, bold-looking flower that can grow up to 30cm (1ft) in height in a week!

- Lamb's Ears (*Stachys byzantine*): it's easy to see how this plant got its common name when you touch the silky foliage.

- Jerusalem Sage (*Phlomis fruticosa*): soft, downy leaves and stems with pretty yellow flowers.

- Curry plant (*Helichrysum italicum*): curry-scented leaves give off a spicy aroma on a warm, sunny day.

- Lavender (*Lavandula angustifolia* 'Hidcote' blue): the classic scent of a summer garden. Cut and dry the flowers for use indoors.

- Chocolate Cosmos (*Cosmos atrosanguineus*): beautiful deep red flowers that give off a chocolate/vanilla scent – bound to be a hit with the children.

- Sweet Pea (*Lathyrus odoratus*): pretty flowering climber that gives off a strong sweet scent. Cut the flowers regularly to encourage more growth.

- Spearmint Plant (*Mentha spicata*): a vigorous growing herb that tastes great with peas or new potatoes!

- Clematis (*General Sikorski*): large and profuse blue/purple flowers.

- Rosemary (*Rosmarinus officinalis*): highly fragrant leaves, used to flavour meat and fish. Plant it in a place where people will brush by and release its scent.

- Nasturtium (*Tropaeolum majus*): it's possible to make a colourful salad from the beautiful, peppery orange, red or yellow flowers of the nasturtium, as well as its foliage.

- Chives (*Allium schoenoprasum*): as well as having delicious foliage that can be used in salads, this plant also produces pretty flowers in pink, mauve or purple.

- Radishes (*Raphanus sativus*): easy to grow and doesn't take long between sowing and reaping.

- Wild Strawberry (*Fragaria vesca*): children will love hunting for the small, sweet, delicious fruit.

- Honeysuckle (*Lonicera Japonica*): a great climber that will give greenery and colour year on year.

- Winter Honeysuckle (*Lonicera fragrantissima*): Gives colour through the winter.

- Heather (*Calluna vulgaris*): low growing perennial ground cover.

The following are trees, bushes and shrubs you might wish to consider:

Some are evergreen (E) and some deciduous (D) — you are advised to select an appropriate mixture of each.

- **Potentilla Fruticosa (D):** Very colourful, compact, low, bushy, plant. Masses of bright buttercup-yellow, saucer-shaped flowers, 1 inch (2.5cm) across, from late spring to mid-autumn, dark green leaves.

- **Silver Birch (Betula Pendula) (D):** A graceful and attractive tree with light airy foliage and distinctive white peeling bark.

- **Golden Privet (Ligustrum Vicaryi) (Semi E):** Soft golden leaves and sprays of pretty white flowers in late spring.

- **Forest Flame (Pieris Japonica) (E):** Glossy brilliant red young leaves gradually turn pink creamy white then dark green. In late spring clusters of pretty ivory nodding bell-like flowers appear resembling lily-of-the-valley.

- **Hydrangea Macrophylla (D):** Medium bush with green leaves and large mop head blue flowers in mid-summer.

- **Silk tree (Albizia julibrissin) (D):** Small tree growing to 5–12 m tall, with a broad crown of level or arching branches. The bark is dark greenish grey in colour and striped vertically as it gets older.

- **Jews Mallow (Nalte Jute) (D):** Bright double yellow flowers and light green oval leaves which can illuminate the shadiest north facing wall or dark corner.

- **Weigela Florida (Red Prince) (D):** Compact, deciduous shrub with creamy margins to its leaves. Pale pink flowers emerge from darker buds in late spring/early summer.

- **Common White Jasmine (Jasminum officiale) (E):** Sweetly scented climber smothered in clusters of highly fragrant white flowers from June to August and pretty, fine green foliage.

- **Cherry Plum Blossom Tree (Sakura) (D):** Flowering tree with blossoms that come out in early spring.

- **Choisya (Ternata Sundance) Mexican orange blossom (E):** Green leaves with groups of small fragrant white flowers in summer and autumn.

Potentilla Fruticosa

Silver Birch

Forest Flame

Hydrangea

- **Bugleweed (Ajuga Bugle) (E):** Great ground cover. Foliage is robust, evergreen and deep purple in colour, and makes a good background to the upright spikes of blue flowers, produced in spring. Very versatile, equally at home as ground cover under trees or shrubs as in a sunny flower border, and even in containers.

- **Acer (Palmatum-osakazuki) (D):** Finely cut leaved Japanese maples. The foliage emerges mid-green in early spring, assuming orange, crimson and purple tints in autumn.

- **Buxus Semperimens (E):** Smaller evergreen shrubs. The leaves are rounded and leathery.

- **Buddleia (Davidii) (D):** Long green and silvery leaves with long purple flowers in summer which attract butterflies.

- **Skimmia Japonica (Rubella) (E):** Medium sized evergreen shrub provides ideal low maintenance evergreen ground cover. Attractive red edged foliage is accompanied by masses of heavily scented red or pink blossom in spring.

- **Viburnum (Davidii) (E):** Medium border plant. Medium green foliage with white flowers in the summer.

- **Smoke Bush (Cotinus Coggygria) (E):** Green and purple leaves. Covered in summer with a smoky haze of soft open flower plumes.

- **Hebe (Eliptica) (E):** A hardy evergreen bushy shrub. The leaves are fleshy, green, and oval, with light edges. The flowers are white to pale mauve.

- **Bamboo (Phyllostachys) (E):** Pretty foliage that 'whispers in the wind while its stems knock together, creating a hollow sound'.

- **Cornus Florida Daybreak (Ornamental tree) (D):** This small deciduous tree has an elegant canopy with spreading, horizontal branches and it flowers in mid-spring, covering itself with upward-facing white blooms.

- **Whitebeam-Sorbus (Aria Lutescens) (D):** Medium sized, deciduous tree that has a naturally upright and rounded canopy. Best features are the silvery grey hairs that cover new leaves and which remain on the underside of the mature leaf.

- **Canadian Maple (Acer rubrum) (D):** 'Scanlon' has a superb red autumn colour and a reasonably narrow, upright habit. The leaves are lush green in the summer months, turning to rich orange and red in the autumn before falling.

Bamboo

White Jasmine

Bugleweed

Buddleia

Skimmia Japonica

Chapter 8

Developing your outdoor area

Outdoor areas come in all shapes and sizes and each in its own way is unique. Unless it is a completely new building/setting it is unlikely that anyone is presented with an outdoor space which is a totally blank canvas.

Four things should be on our mind when we first look at any outdoor space.

1   Is it safe and secure for children?

2   Is it stimulating?

3   What will children gain from engagement with the area?

4   How can it be improved to meet the needs of the children?

So it shouldn't be…
'What is my dream for the space?'

But rather
'What do our children need from it?'

Nor…
'What will look really impressive?'

But rather
'What will maximise children's learning and development outcomes?'

Or…
'I want it just like the fabulous one up the road that I've seen.' But rather 'What we develop will be unique and different and will meet the needs of our children and community.'

1 Ensuring the area is safe and secure

One of the first things that needs to be attended to is to make the area safe and secure for the children and where possible well fenced so as to keep any vandals out who will trash the nice things you have created.

- Gates should always be securely bolted from inside and/or locked once children have access to these. It should not be a route of entry for staff or parents who are on a late shift or who arrive late.

- Bushes, trees or plants which are unsuitable and/or dangerous should be removed unless these are fenced off in a wild area where children will only access when appropriately supervised by practitioners e.g laburnum trees, roses, blackberry bushes.

- Any doors leading from the building are risk assessed and action taken to ensure these do not blow shut and/or trap children's hands etc. It may be necessary or advisable to fit finger safe edging strips.

- Ensure that staffing levels are such that the area is appropriately supervised. This will depend on the ages/stages of the children and the identified needs of the children.

Welfare outdoors

The welfare of children is both supported and challenged by outdoor learning.

Children need to be safe and secure when outdoors. Any perimeter fencing needs to be tall enough to prevent children being lifted over and abducted, and ideally children will be able to see through the fence. Additionally taller fencing helps to deter would-be vandals entering the area.

Outdoor spaces need to be checked regularly before and during sessions and any litter or dangerous things like glass, needles, animal faeces etc removed. The following audit can be utilised to ensure that welfare requirements relating to outdoors are in place and understood by all the staff team.

Outdoor Welfare Monitoring Audit

Area	Evidence	Not in place	Partly in place	Fully in place	Monitored by
A: Safeguarding	Early identification of children at risk is made and appropriate responses to this information are provided by the setting	●	○	●	
Setting has identified children with a low level of engagement and participation and appropriate/effective responses are made and recorded - indoors and outdoors.					
Behaviour management policy is in place and appropriately implemented in line with children's needs and stage of development outdoors.					
Outdoor spaces are made safe and kept safe from intruders. Regular checks are made and these are recorded.					
Staff all aware of Safeguarding Vulnerable Groups Act 2006 and possible signs of concerns.					

Area	Evidence	Not in place	Partly in place	Fully in place	Monitored by
B: Suitable People	All those who work with children meet the EYFS requirements in terms of qualifications and experience and ratios at all times.	●	○	●	
All staff are enhanced CRB checked and records are kept which are regularly updated — this includes all regular visitors with access to children and supply staff.					
All staff receive ongoing training to support implementation of the EYFS welfare requirements. Where there are identified staff needs these are met through additional training and support.					
Staff hold appropriate levels of qualifications, experience skills and knowledge in line with EYFS requirements.					
The organisation of staff and clarity of their roles ensures children's ongoing safety and the meeting of their needs outdoors.					
Staff ratios are in line with or better than EYFS requirements at all times indoors and outdoors.					

OUTDOOR WELFARE MONITORING AUDIT   Copyright The Early Years Consultancy Ltd 2011   www.theearlyyearsconsultancy.com

Area	Evidence	Not in place	Partly in place	Fully in place	Monitored by
C: Premises, environments equipment and resources	The premises and equipment enable children to learn and develop in a safe and supportive environment	●	○	○	
Daily safety and fit for purpose checks are made in the outdoor area/s and these are recorded.					
Outdoor area is secure against intruders and regular monitoring checks are made.					
Equipment and resources outdoors are appropriate to children's stages of development and are stored in appropriately accessible ways for children.					
Children are provided with regular daily physical exercise indoors/ outdoors.					
Equipment and resources are appropriately maintained in clean and safe condition and regularly replenished as necessary (e.g. sand in outdoor sand pit).					
Environment outdoors is maintained free from litter and rubbish and is kept tidy, weed free and is generally well cared for.					

OUTDOOR WELFARE MONITORING AUDIT   Copyright The Early Years Consultancy Ltd 2011   www.theearlyyearsconsultancy.com

Area	Evidence	Not in place	Partly in place	Fully in place	Monitored by
D: Documentation	Records are appropriate, secure, easily accessible and kept up to date	●	○	●	
Information is obtained (and regularly kept updated) from parents as to any allergies medication and any other that is important and relevant.					
EYFS policies relating to outdoor learning are in place.					
Daily routines and procedures for outdoor learning opportunities are prominently displayed and appropriately shared with parents/carers and reviewed on a regular basis including key person role.					
Risk assessments are undertaken for any identified dangers and risks and these are written up. This includes any trips or visits made outside of the school.					
Insurance is taken out for all children going on trips/visits prior to the trip and signed permissions from parents/carers are obtained prior to the trip/visit.					

OUTDOOR WELFARE MONITORING AUDIT   Copyright The Early Years Consultancy Ltd 2011   www.theearlyyearsconsultancy.com

Area	Evidence	Not in place	Partly in place	Fully in place	Monitored by
D: Documentation	Records are appropriate, secure, easily accessible and kept up to date	●	○	○	
Trips are well planned to ensure any essential records are taken (e.g. emergency contact numbers, medical notes), essential medication, mobile phone with credit and charge, and names of those on the trip are noted in the setting's registers in case of fire etc.					
Children's developmental records are maintained and updated on a regular ongoing basis and progress regularly shared with parents/carers. These include observations from outdoors.					
Children at risk of underachievement are identified and their needs met through short term planning and provision indoors and outdoors.					
Planning for outdoors is clear, purposeful and appropriately differentiated to meet children's needs and stages of development.					
Information is provided for parents on the value and benefits of outdoor learning.					
Equality policy includes how the needs of all children will be met indoors and outdoors.					

Area	Evidence	Not in place	Partly in place	Fully in place	Monitored by
E: Illness, infection and accidents	Records are appropriate, secure, easily accessible and kept up to date	●	○	●	
Effective procedures are in place for children who are taken ill and parents/carers are contacted as soon as possible.					
Effective procedures are in place for children who are injured/hurt during sessions indoors and outdoors including use of an accident book where all accidents are appropriately recorded and later shared with parents.					
Accidents outdoors are reviewed to ascertain any trends and need to improve practice or provision.					
F: Food and drink					
Water is always readily available for children to access.					
Children are regularly reminded and helped to wash their hands before eating and/or after outdoor play.					
Food hygiene and health and safety requirements are adhered to at all times including at snack times.					
Children are supported to understand the importance of physical exercise.					

OUTDOOR WELFARE MONITORING AUDIT   Copyright The Early Years Consultancy Ltd 2011   www.theearlyyearsconsultancy.com

2 Ensuring the area offers appropriate stimulation

As a team, led by the EYFS leader, practitioners need to assess how the area can offer activities which will inspire and motivate the children to achieve towards the early learning goals in all six areas of learning.

Initially it is best to start with two audits of:

(A) Which areas are already appropriately developed and useable e.g roadway

(B) What resources exist which are, or can be specifically, for use outdoors. In some cases there is already an outdoor storage shed or container which is full of a range of items from trikes and trailers to balls and hoops.

These resources and equipment need to be assessed as…

- needing to be discarded immediately due to being unsafe or unsuitable or not cost effective to repair.

- having limited life left in them and in need of replacement as soon as possible.

- items which are suitable, safe and usefully support learning and development. At this point it is no use being other than honest with ourselves and keeping things that are of little use or which are dangerous. It is the time to get rid and start as we mean to go on.

NB: Once these audits have taken place you can then see what you have in place and from this decide what is required. It is always good to take photos at this point to remind you where you were up to and as evidence of how it used to be before it was improved.

Having completed the audits you need to decide what action is required and the timescale for this. Often there are funding implications which will lead to a time gap of at least a few months or maybe a few years before any major work can be undertaken. At this point don't just sit back and wait as you need to think about the children currently attending. So you should sit down and decide what you can do:

(i) **Immediately** – over the next few weeks and which will cost a minimum or no cost at all.

(ii) **In the shorter term** – over the next few months which cost a smaller amount of money and which can be later fitted in to the overall planned development.

(iii) **In the longer term** – over the next year or more (big vision). This will be the major costing of the development of sustainable developed outdoor provision areas. The plan should be discussed and consulted upon with staff, governors/management committee, children and parents.

Consideration should be given to the existing trends of data of children's achievements/development over the previous three years, with specific attention given to those areas where many children are not achieving due to the limitations of what is currently on offer.

It may not be possible to undertake/complete the whole of the 'big vision' in one step and therefore it may be necessary to plan to complete it in two or three phases. Here there will be a fine balance between prioritising children's needs and available funding and deciding what will be undertaken in each phase.

(i), (ii) and (iii) should each take into account 'What will children gain from engagement with the area as it exists currently?' and 'How can it be improved to meet the needs of the children?'

A major hurdle is getting a price that you can afford and a contractor who will do a job that lasts for many years without falling apart. Remember…

- the cheapest price is not always the best price (although it can be sometimes)

- it is best to use contractors whose work you can visit and see the quality of for yourself – ideally try to get someone recommended by others

- to ensure you have worded the contract so that what you think you are getting is what is actually being supplied

- always ask for a guarantee that the work meets the required safety standards and that they will return to finish any snags you have found before you pay the full amount

- it is best to get at least three quotes for the work. Always get the quotation in writing (not an estimate) and then be prepared to negotiate. I have always found the price quoted leaves room for this!

- contractors will often try to persuade you to have things that they make the most profit from – some of which were not in your original design or were not envisaged in that way!

The following case studies are examples of settings who have gone through a similar process to this. They have moved on to develop outdoor environments which have made a difference to the lives of children by helping to improve their learning and development outcomes. The purpose of these case studies is to provide visual and descriptive examples of the process involved in developing an outdoor area.

Always remember that your outdoor space/area is unique and your children will have different needs from those in the case studies. Hence what you develop will be for these reasons uniquely different.

Case Study 1

The newly acquired outdoor space.

Kids Unlimited Day Nursery

Set in the grounds of the Countess of Chester Hospital, this day nursery had a somewhat limited space which the manager felt could be developed to offer much more varied and exciting learning opportunities. Mainly laid with grass, some hard surfacing was added in the form of concrete flagging adjacent to the access doors. A large outdoor sandpit was provided to support a variety of activities from treasure hunts to making sandcastles.

An area where grass was allowed to grow tall was incorporated and logs were added but the gardeners still have to be reminded not to cut the long grass as they have done in past. A structure was built with flagging to the front which is utilised for group times. This offers some shade and shelter and has lots of potential uses including a performing arts area.

Soft surfacing has recently been laid to an area to one side of the building and this area is used for balancing and crawling activities using portable resources/equipment.

The supply of water was an issue and although a small water butt was available the setting also added a water tap, set at child height, which proved very useful indeed.

A willow dome was constructed which provided an enclosed secure space for role-play and other activities and also provided an additional group time space.

A wooden shed was sourced and erected and this was targeted to allow safe storage, accessible during the sessions for children to select and put away their own resources.

The large grassy area which is well drained was retained with a hilly aspect being introduced so that it offered more challenge and interest.

Two swings were set up which allowed younger children to be securely fastened in and to enjoy the exhilaration of swinging backwards and forwards.

Alongside this a natural and growing area was provided with a mini plastic zip up covered growing frame. Tomatoes are propagated in growing bags along a sheltered south facing wall.

PVC guttering was positioned along the wooden fence at an angle. This provided opportunities for balls to be rolled down or water to be poured along.

Also provided were large mark making boards and boards where paper could be attached for large scale painting and drawing.

In the central area, in front of the wooden fencing, is a space dedicated to role-play as a building site. This area is used by children from aged 18 months to five years.

There are additional dedicated outdoor spaces for babies and for toddlers.

An outdoor resource shelf is filled each day with outdoor resource boxes. This is handily sited on the flagged area close to the access doors to the area allowing for children to select the resources they require.

On the grassy area, climbing opportunities are provided through a 'Little Tykes' portable framework and planks are used across the hills to support imaginative play.

Swings for the very young.

Outdoor tap - a small cost but a huge benefit!

Overall, there is always a wide range of interesting and exciting learning opportunities on offer whatever the weather as the setting has a range of outdoor suits to fit children from toddlers though to pre-schoolers. Weather does not stop learning at Kids Unlimited in Chester! The quality of the outdoor provision at this setting was acknowledged and recognised by a recent Ofsted inspection as outstanding.

However, this setting is always on the look out to make the provision better including adding more outdoor space whenever the opportunity arises. The photo opposite shows the latest acquisition of extra space created following negotiation with the site management. Originally it was a small border area of bushes just outside the nursery fencing. This has been fenced in and soft surfaced as an area for the toddler room to have a space of their own with continuous availability throughout the day. Already there are strawberries being grown in grow bags and sensory plants and herbs in pots in a mini herb garden. Large scale painting and mark making is also made available along with water play with gutters, pipes and funnels. New developments are being made/added daily.

Making music with kitchen resources.

Soft surfacing for balancing, crawling and other activities.

The large outdoor sandpit — a great asset for learning and development.

Guttering set at an angle along the fencing.

The herb garden and strawberries.

The outdoor building site role play.

Case Study 2

View across the area before re-development.

St James CE Primary School, Gorton, Manchester

In the autumn of 2009 funding was found to develop the very poor outdoor space attached to the early years building at St James CE Primary School. This was a long mainly tarmaced space with some muddy patches, a few large trees, a large climbing frame and an old veranda with a leaking roof and very little else. Overall it offered very little stimulation and was failing to support the children's learning and development. I was brought in to create a design brief and to work with the staff and children to ensure this met the indentified needs and interests of the children. Additionally, the school wanted their Year one pupils to be able to use the area for some parts of the day.

The project was started by looking at the past three years data to identify what the children in this community needed. Children's ideas were gathered and then initial plans drawn up and presented/discussed at a governor's meeting. Parents were also invited to comment and provide ideas on the proposals. The design brief identified in Chapter 4 of this book was used and a finalised plan drawn up which then went out to tender.

Completed in the autumn term of 2010 the result was a superb play area where children's learning and welfare needs were met. The shuttered veranda which runs along most of the building's access to the outdoor space ensures that storage of resources and equipment overnight is facilitated and that shade and shelter were always available. The outcomes for the children have shown a significant improvement already and it is envisaged that greater things are yet to come!

The re-development has provided much more stimulating and engaging provision. The school is still developing some further aspects including the portable resources.

The long covered, shuttered veranda facilitating water play, a sand pit and much more.

Adventure area.

The open-ended wooden imaginative play structure.

The new, large ball/running area.

Raised vegetable growing beds alongside the new roadway.

Case Study 3

The dilapidated building which was demolished.

Ringway Pimary School, Wythenshawe, Manchester

In the spring of 2006 there was agreement by the Senior Management Team at the school that unless the outdoor area at Ringway Primary School was further developed then outcomes for children would be severely limited. I was brought in by the school to design the space and to help monitor its implementation. The outdoor area had already been partly developed several years previously. There was the opportunity for further space to be added with the proposed demolition of some single storey unused and dilapidated classrooms. This would provide space for a turfed area and additional garden space to be added.

The sitting reading and gathering area.

Overview of the raised planting area.

Growing vegetables can support all areas of learning.

A much improved roadway area with new planting.

The new long willow tunnel – an exciting feature for the children that's over 10 metres long!

Case Study 4

Old Hall Drive Primary School, Manchester

Old Hall Drive Primary School is set in inner city Gorton, Manchester. The area outside the nursery was always well used by the children but was an unusually long, narrow shape which had previously had development but lacked the required quality expected by the EYFS guidance framework. So two years ago a creative and visionary Head teacher decided things had to change and it did! Through a cleverly designed, quality development the area now has a new storage container which can be accessed directly through a side door.

The space for the children has among other things:

- a space in which a range of vegetables are grown

- a covered gathering area with a story teller's chair and children's seating

- an improved roadway

- fixed chalking boards

- several seater planters

- a ball/running area with appropriate low fencing

- an outdoor sand pit

- a natural area with trees and mirrors and benches

- a climbing area.

Overall it has not only proved to be a great success with the children and parents/carers who really love it but it has helped to secure improved outcomes for children.

The quality of this provision was acknowledged in a recent HMI/Ofsted inspection of the school. However, not too long afterwards the innovative Head teacher at the school recognised that more needed to be done to secure continuous outdoor learning for the Reception children who were sharing the nursery area which...

(a) wasn't big enough for 4 classes and

(b) was not available continuously due to the Reception classes being on the other side of the school.

A covered story teller chair and seating circle with the new storage container in the

The natural area with trees, bushes, mirrors and a buddy bench.

Soft surfacing for balancing, crawling and other activities.

Seater planters and a chalk board.

The climbing area now enclosed and safe from the roadway vehicles or the footballs!!

So in the summer of 2011 she commissioned a new outdoor area to be built using part of the school yard outside the Reception classes. Again, this has been a resounding success down to innovation and creative thinking. Reception children can still share the nursery area for a short part of the day - to access areas of provision like the roadway, the ball running area and the large climbing frame - but now have their own space designed and built specially for them. This includes:

- A sandpit

- A trim trail

- Covered seating area

- Story teller's chair and seating

- Traversing tower

- Mirror

- Wall mounted mark making boards

- Mini bamboo water structure

What next one wonders at a school that never stops thinking how to improve their EYFS provision?

The outdoor building site role play.

The trim trail.

Marked area for ball games.

Bibliography and further reading

Abbott L and Langston A (2005) *Birth to Three Matters: Supporting the framework of effective practice.* Open University Press

Bilton, H (2002) *Outdoor Play in the Early Years.* David Fulton Publishers

Bilton, H (2004) *Playing Outside.* David Fulton Publishers

Bruce and Meggitt, (1999) *Child Care And Education.* Hodder Arnold

Edgington, M (2003) *The Great Outdoors.* BAECE

Edgington, M (2002) *The Nursery Teacher in Action.* Sage Publications

Featherstone, S (2003) *The Little Book of Outside In All Weathers.* Featherstone Education, Bloomsbury Publishing

Gould, T. (2011) *The Fabulous Early Years Foundation Stage.* Featherstone Education, Bloomsbury Publishing

Jarman, E (2010) *A Place to talk Outside.* Featherstone Education, Bloomsbury Publishing

Knight, S (2009) *Forest Schools And Outdoor Learning In The Early Years.* Sage Publications

Louv, R (2009) *Last Child In the Woods.* Atlantic Books

Ouvry, M (2000) *Exercising Muscles And Minds.* National Early Years Network

Roberts, A. (2011) *The Little Book of Minibeast Hotels* Featherstone Education, Bloomsbury Publishing

Ryder Richardson, G (2006) *Creating A Space To Grow.* David Fulton Publishers

White, J (2009) *Playing And Learning Outdoors.* Routledge